ALONG THE WAY
Poems from a Life Journey

Fred B. Newton

****

D1260537

ALONG THE WAY

Table of Contents

PART 1: FUN WITH WORDS

Sometimes it is just fun to be playful with sound, alliteration, and the juxtaposition of words. I have always enjoyed e.e. cummings as the master for marrying ideas through words and images! I am not a Cummings, but I like to have "fun with words." This section follows my attempts to engage with a "tongue in cheek" peak at life.

to be *nobody but yourself* – in a world which is doing its best, night and day, to make you everybody else – means to fight the hardest battle which any human being can fight; and never stop fighting.

e.e. cummings

Leaky Blotchy Ink Spots

Leaky pen
spews its careless ink...
splotch
blot words.

Shhh don't tell!!!
The trickle which
oozes
upon this page
could betray a spark
from an inner flame,
a zap-brief flicker.

Inky spots linger,
as an indelible residue,
a black goo
from another day,
footprints of a past moment
irrevocably etched to a future
where stuffed sparks
may be squelched.

"Deny" you say...
but are even small
flickers extinguished?
or are they hidden

lights of hope,
blips of memory,
ergs to build a new and
potentially lasting bond?

Intuition

In-toot the Ute,
shun the ignition,
it's time to use
your intuition.

When you begin to worry,
grumble inside,
it's the inside demon
catching a lie.

You can use the words
with explanation deep,
but nothing compares
with the soundless peep.

Grab a wave length
better hold on tight,
as you take off
on a rollercoaster flight.

Sometimes you are up,
Sometimes your down,
Occasionally your feet
May touch the ground.

But given a choice
I'd rather in-too-it,
Than live the other way
Of think then do-it.

Glued to Paper

Jon: Why do you clutch so tightly latching on with a suffocating hold that allows so little freedom?

Sal: What do you expect me to do? As I sit all day immersed in myself to the point of screaming...as you lay before me. So white open!

Jon: Can I have your attachment without the screaming expectation to hold close as you experience coming unglued?

Sal: Attachment is my "sole" reason to be!

Jon: Is it possible to stick only slightly, keep you grounded in one piece without letting go?

Sal: But, you protest my adherence and constancy while you benefit the most without stapled frazzled edges that are no longer torn!

Written with partner at Alanon Writer's Workshop, Big Sur, CA

Anaphora for an Anemone

It seems quite an enigma
to write an ode to a nematode,
especially when I am more prone
to sing praises to an anemone.

However, an anomalous gnome
may be suffering at home,
having pangs of anomie
uncured by the flushing of an enema.

Oh dear, I have great fear
when speaking anonymously of anemia
the anaphora of this verse
will make my condition much worse.

So, I must stop going on
forever and anon,
when my Jungian anima
longs for my lovely anemone.

FROG POWER

May the power of the frog

cleanse you,

as the gentle rains of life

soothe your way.

And may you gain new meaning

from a lily pad's repose

to replenish your strength

by hopping over a sludge

filled day,

surrounded and nourished

by a pond of goodness!

A NAUGHTY mouse

PICKLED pucker among
PLENTOUS PACKAGES of unforgotten PLUS,

I dreamt of a GNOME who carried WHISPERING
Love letters to US.

While FRETTING and FUMING about
a FAIRLY young FANNY...
he Fell FLAT on his FRITTERING flus!

And now those GNOME LIVERED cheese FLAVORED
notes are being sent via GREYHOUND bus.

By a FAIRLY NICE guy who remains
A NAUGHTY-MOUSE!

Woodland Sprite

Who is this crazy woodland sprite?
living life in playful pixie ways,
with roller blades and flying kites,
and sleepy morning beyond the night.

She eats desserts before her meals,
laughs with glee when playing tricks,
and gets a kick from the look she steals,
a tongue-in-cheek of the way she feels.

Sometimes she gets to feeling bad
and makes herself all small and "puny",
but rather than staying down and sad
she receives gifts and flowers to make her glad.

The woman is such a delight to be found
bringing joy and fun into each day of my life,
with a snooze alarm, toys and beds abound,
oh dear, I love it, that you are around!

Quirky and Loopy

Quirky and Loopy were two goats that found each other in a world filled with cats, dogs, humanoids, and a few wolves. They would wake up each morning and laugh out loud at this funny universe in which they lived because goats have a whole different perspective on the way "things" may be.

For example, goats like to brush up against each other, sometimes even bump heads, scratch each other's back, and rub oil on their bodies. They even try to make pretzels and knots by entangling their bodies with each other. This is a form of sculpture that is particularly indigenous to goats.

Also, goats will often make comments, somewhat tongue in cheek (which is not to say the same thing as tongue in mouth) when they see discrepancies. For example, at the doctor's office the nurse measured the loopy goat and found she was a half inch taller than the previous year. Loopy exclaimed, "wow...I have grown a whole half inch", quite an unusual feat for an adult goat. The nurse was quick to say "no, no this is just a measurement error". The nurse was quite naive to think that a loopy goat was that naïve and was just being humorous. You see dogs, cats and humanoids in this world are much more serious and literal in their thinking.

Goats like to make sounds that seem to reflect their mood and often mock the tone-ations of their surrounds. "Baaa" is just one of those sounds, but they also grunt, and use words like "whoops", "wow", "far out", and get excited when they see a real "pop stand". Even more peculiar they frequently break into songs, often made up in the spare of the moment, that emulate very serious musicals and operas, which reflect life stories. In fact, when they encounter a humanoid that has unique characteristics, gestures, or make unusual impressions-- they find it quite easy to make up a life story to explain what is going on in that person's life. These explanations are usually more interesting than the so called "real story" (which, of course, is only itself something that the person has made up to explain themselves).

Humans, as well as dogs and cats, do a lot to posture themselves in a "good light". For example, there was the rule bound and tight assed principal of a school that needed to declare public ally that he was a liberal. This very much resembled the attempt of the proverbial wolf who tried to make appearance as a sheep. This certainly makes any goat worth his (or her) salt to take notice of the two headed/two faced qualities present with many of these so-called civilized humans. But, I must not digress into unusual because the goats themselves take pride in being unusual, unique, and having a more playful view of life.

The end.

My "Am"

I am who I am
because I am,
but sometimes I am afraid
to be who I am.

I want to say, please know
what you may have seen
as I was open
has not changed who I am.

Who I am goes inside,
a frightened but sheltered am
protected, but also lost
from my friends
who I am.

If I loved,
I still love not showing you
who I am
does not mean that
I am not there.

Only temporarily enclosed
until my am dares
to disclose again.
Hope you are still there,
I am!

SUBTLE MESSAGES

The trouble with WORDS
is what they don't say.
Yet, I have not learned to trust
my *in-touch* with you,
pure-state UNIVERSE
conveyed through time/space
more efficient means.

Therefore, this inefficient LETTER
arrives well after the MESSAGE was sent.
As you might have guessed
the meaning is not in these words
but, more like a kiss STAMPED
upon this page...

which will be felt as a warmth which
envelopes
You!

DIALOG WITH THUNDERCLOUD

A booming voice claps violently down from above!

"You are an old voice, I know from the past!"
  Yes, I have always been with you.

"But, I can hardly see your image"
  It is because it is not my image you seek,
  as I am your deep voice.

"but, where are you?"
  I am where you plumb the depths
  below the surface of the water, or
  in patterns of a bird's flight, or with
  the resonance when you listen in stillness.

"Listen to what is still?"
  Yes, still as in listen quietly.

"With my ears?"
  No, with your ancient heart.

"Am I making you up in my imagination?"
  Yes, I am made up just as you are an image,
  what are we without imagination?

"What can you teach me?"
  What do you want to know?

"I want to meet and interact with a large animal."
  You must speak in a voice that it understands.

"A bear can growl and grab my attention to listen!"
  As ants can move mountains in silence!

PART 2: THE FOUR SEASONS

A metaphor for the changing environments of life is to experience the four seasons and recognize the variations and flow that derive. This section collects a range of my thoughts over my life that seem to relate to the "seasons of life."

AUTUMN LAYERS

A swoosh of cool breeze butterflies my face
followed by lingering warm layers,
ambivalent promises of a
summer's passage.

Mixed messages of autumn toasting
burnt brown, yellow, orange
flavored with a vivid flair
of burgundy mums.

A few moments reflect of days past
before hurried preparations for the
hearty demands of grey/white
frost biting future.

WINTER'S BRIEF MOMENTS

My breath gasped for a piece of air,
       my eyes blurred
       from the sudden rush of an ascending winter wind.
Can one prepare for this sudden change of season?

A snowflake stroked with the essence
       of a completely new pattern
       touched the tip of my nose,
       warmed to a droplet,
then disappeared in a cloud of vapor.

I thought of making new friends
       forming new dimensions
       with the brush of each new crystal,
       lasting the briefest of moments;
       clear, exposed, tickling my nose,
splashing my face with new life.

Meanwhile, an old leaf
       lies decayed under foot,
       slowly holding on to a semblance
of the former self-then dust.

I celebrate with you the renewal of the brief
       yet ever changing moments
       which lie before us,
       vulnerable, yet full
of all that there IS!

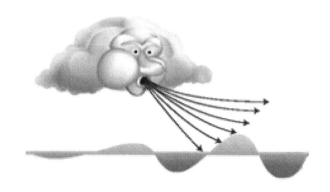

MARCH

Tooth in claw winds blow blurring
    eyes that wince to escape
        the tenacious grip of an
            almost sleeping white giant.

Yet, peeking out from its bed
    warmed by a blanket of leaves
        and sun rays
            from a gentler day.

Stands a daffodil, golden against
    the grayness that is surrounded
        by a bleak and turbulent
            exit of lioness March.

Another winter retreats
    through not so subtle noise
        hammering out warnings
            of tornadic spring.

But also, a promise of sunny rooms
with growing plants,
and boisterous boys
with tousled blonde hair
and mud cake hands;

That pluck the faerae yellow bud
at throats length to
offer as a sacrifice
or a mothering one.

SPRING'S FLIRTATION

Steps along a garden path,
shredded leaves from a winter's frost,
musty odor of a new forming earth's
awakening.

As a hummingbird's hesitation
a maiden skirt sways from cirrus wisps
that glide and evaporate clear as eidetic
memory.

An elusive essence mingles
with lone pipsissewa blossom
from its winter coat
peaking.

The flirtation of earthen woman,
In holographic guile,
playing butterfly with the sense of
Spring.

The Web

Today,

    I saw the bloom of new earth

    the breeze of fresh air,

    the promise of newness in life.

And a cobweb

    nimbly anchored to bush,

    waived against a morning blue

    issuing subtle ominous warning to the passerby.

A fly

    struggles to free itself from an entangled bed

    each effort becomes more hopeless.

    Reaching forward to help the creature—

No!

    It must make its own struggle

    reaching freedom or death alone.

The err

      of the web was earned.

      It's struggles penitence justifiable,

      its despair is tragedy in life,

      and freedom earned is the hope and reward

      one savors as his own.

I, too.

Part 3: THE EXISTENTIAL MOMENT

Perspective, philosophy, beliefs or musings about meaning and the nature of life are the theme for these writings. This section contains poems that were written at many different moments of life.

Birds of a Feather

The Life OF MOSES

You see I am not so certain
in my traveling way
of places to go or
wanting to stay.

A nibble or two
a taste of life,
then turn around to
avoid the strife.

I sample the gift of
possibility,
but recognize a choice
is less than nobility.

My usual purpose is to
leave a mark,
a contribution left
without the spark.

A conservative messenger
between two places,
dares not to enter either
with warm embraces.

A man like Moses
guides people by the hand,
but after life in the desert
eats only grapes of the land.

At points of frustration
he angrily strikes the rock,
only to learn it is better,
to take a humbler walk.

Years after leading a life
of cautious running,
he might choose to enter
that land of milk and honey!

STAR GAZE

A star wanders through darkness

of a vast universe sky

and twinkles to my gaze,

facing upward from a bed of snow.

A cold clear night silenced to all,

Yet the sound of Pegasus

the great winged horse,

brings a current to me,

a minute speck in a greater fabric.

I have only to listen,

only to hear,

only to ride the current of my destiny

without need for effort

into a timeless expanse of energy.

Tapestry

Human forces
joined to form
a simple
woven rug
with frayed
edges
and irregular
surfaces.

A unique
blending of
fabric
with hues
reflecting
an array of
shadow and
light.

A spectrum of
color and
texture
merged as one
to become a
piece of art.

ROUGH EDGES

Hewn in sinewy chunks
   that form MASS,
Defined and purposeful.

Yet, also an unfinished work
   with
IN-
  com-
   PLETE-
    ness
betraying the uneasy
     SENSE
that final line and polish
    depicts a portrayal,
susceptible
   to critique,
   GOOD/BAD that is.

Thus, suspended in almost
     READY STATE,
I await your final
   TOUCH.

28

Twilight State

Happenings in twilight state;
a dreamy gift promised on a day six months ago.
A return to the blue horizon with happy waves
on the shores of my soul.

Connected to a place, no a space,
more like a collective group
of molecules, some more than others,
warm, squishy, sleepy, alive!

A blue bird snatches a blue berry,
a cat wishes for cream,
my wife snuggles beside me,
I am having a dream.

Of buses, doors, and little boy toys—
of rescuers and persecutors.
They are all "one" and all "none".
As the images become dark, but the sound
never stops resonating in my ears.

Aging you say, but I remember the years
and the thoughts.
I see it all, I see it not at all—
just a snatch, I must escape to isolation
to comprehend and get my "wind"
by breathing the thin air
and sharing the lingering moments with you!

Interlude

The interface of light and dark,

the blending into shades of each.

We share all without judgement

and experience the ultimate uniqueness.

A sensation of belonging, an interlude becomes a paradox

where we become one in knowing and being,

Time stands still and yet we experience its passing

with new awareness hitherto unknown,

surpassing previous understanding.

Meaningless words have meaning,

and silence says everything.

An interlude proceeds as the shared moment,

that merges present, past and future as one.

When, by chance or measure this happens,

we accept the now.

And when it ends the essence lingers on as a reality

Until another interlude may be shared, again!

REALITY?

CLARITY,
The pure essence of knowing and being at one
where experience is now...
uncontaminated by the grays of worry,
and the uncertainties and insecurities that creep in
making an atmosphere filled with clouds of doubt—
For what is real-ity?

CLARITY,
Where the sky is blue to an infinitesimal depth
and the experience is grasped with the
fullest means possible.
Where each receptor of the body is in contact
with the adjoining, connecting spheres of life—
extended cells that move on
throughout the universe.

ILLUSIONS,
The fantasies, wishes and desires that
create a hope for reality;
a dream world of possibility,
But, also a cautionary potential for distortion
of the intact, purity of what IS now.
Beware to let the dream clouds part
to make the real be perceptible through
the eyes of the organism.

ILLUSIONS,
Only a template to lead on forward
toward the ideal.
A mountain's destination, a soul-mates relationship,
a correction of error in the maker of reality;
ourselves.

FUSION,
To overlay the template on the reality
without losing the now from the desired,
but knowing the difference.
Where one becomes the guide, the hoped for,
to accept or escape a reality
without diminishment of what IS.

REALITY,
The "IS" may exceed a grand fantasy
with an unending potential in depth
and openness to experience the adjoined
without the distortion throughout
the whole of the universe—
Which, you know, includes and IS you!
I hope for the opportunity to
know you in that way.

PRISM
Musings of a Therapist

Where will an encounter find connection
    at a sudden crucible depth?
A place, any place...you begin
    unfolding pages of different shapes and sizes.
Pages that would hardly fit a book,
    for a person story has no beginning or ending.
Only a being whose surface enters at any point.

A prism of many sides; distinct transparent,
    at different times refracting a light into moods and colors.
Your presence softens a space
    with warm tunic shirt and boots like furry glove.
A face with gently etched, firmly set lines
    that curb a tear reaching to appear and becomes resolute.
A well of beauty remains
    missing the liquid smile of joy.

A romantic...
    touring English country sides on bicycle of love-making frolic,
    a creative bread baker, candlestick maker,
    a scholar, a sometime lawyer and maybe there's more.
Today is for sorting of men and moves,
    places so near, yet further than a turtle reaches
    in a lifetime search for a secure home
    (which it carries unbeknown).
Where will you go? Will a part be missing there?

Rainbow light created through crystal
    shadowed by responsibility of collapsing lives
    crying for your help!
    Mothers, brothers, lovers needing you.
"Is it ok to need to be needed?"
    A humpty dumpty repair service putting parts together again.
Is it alright for you who waited for others through
    break-ups, salvage, business as usual, again?
Is it alright for you to gain a respite and mend oneself?

No! You hear announcements and pronouncements...
    "without funds", "no space for your right".
A voice wonders, can they not hear your cry?
    Do you not speak loud enough?
    Does speaking or hearing not make a difference?
"I scream", you say, "but not here..."

You are here, I am here in this square room
    with two windows of light
    focused for a while.

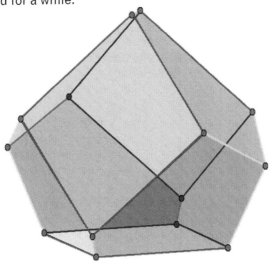

Still Pictures

I am only beginning to be aware
that my awareness is beginning,
not with boundaries defined
all around me,
but with possibilities imaginable.

The truth be known
may not be truth at all,
just pictures taken one day,
repeated the next,
and expected to remain
permanent!

However, new pictures
capture new realities,
truer than before
(although not necessarily).

Discoveries excite me!
To share that excitement
with someone who dares listen
stimulates further ripples of exhilaration,
and yet another set of pictures still.

Ah oh Feelings!

A little pang,
a gnawing, knowing, churning
when one feels the danger
of venturing close,
yet wonders if they are still
alone.

Maybe, you have left that space
or felt the singe of fire
that burns too hot and
backed away
to stay safe.

Or, perhaps it is my
own sensitive too thin skin
that warns of danger
from outside,
which feels an ache to avoid
a larger pain within.

The "ah-oh" wants to go away
but act with caution when a
blank look or distant stare,
hopes a smile will surface,
when the phone rings!

A voice sounds as though I'm sick
or distant you say,
but how can I tell you,
when you had gone away,
I knew you would not
be back again.

Person Centered Credo

Can you accept my sense of aloneness and separateness without seeking to assuage that loneliness by crowding into my space?

Can you tolerate my sense of helplessness without thinking you need to help?

Can you experience my hurt and shame, peeking from behind doors and strong trees, and allow a measure of love and support to enter my soul without scaring the frightened child within?

Can you be patient with my confusion and uncertainty that cries out for direction and retreats without listening for answers?

Can you accept and experience the mysteries of attraction and sexuality while openly sorting and owning with me the conflicts in my motivation?

Can you observe the forces of power and control and with aikido move that energy toward constructive potential?

Can you join another family and not need to change or adapt it to make yourself more comfortable, but just experience the qualities it offers?

Can you trust the love of a friend to be with you even if s/he is loving another?

Can you leave your protected place to walk among us without needing constant signs of affection, respect, or attention to prevent a retreat into solitude?

Can You be a significant force in one moment and a humble servant in the next staying open to both the learning and the teaching?

Can you trust the collective resource of a community to transfer a black cloud of hurt and anger into a candle of enlightenment?

The above quiz was a result of my experience with the Person-Centered Renewal Workshop in Gainesville, Georgia. My answer to this quiz included: yes, sometimes, maybe, and I don't know! The important learning seemed to lie with the clarity of the questions.

PEBBLE ON A BEACH

The pebble lies upon a beach
  surrounded by a million other rocks.
    Unique by color, shape, and substance.
     Each one different in subtle,
       distinguishing characteristics
        from all the rest.

Being a chosen stone carry
  the privilege of standing out;
    A feeling of being selected, honored
     and dignified as a
      special one!

Or, does it mean discernment?
  Is the choice of a seeker
    only a matter of timing and beguilement?
     Fool's gold, the lucky grasp of a moment's reach
      or the true discovery of precious metal?

One cherishes the opportunity to be noticed and known
  be it glitter or substance.
    However, what is the benefit,
     caught up in a sense of worth
      solely on the uncertain reality
       of another's choice?

Let me walk on in my life
   sharing the true colors of my nature.
      If you bring me close
         to nestle in your pocket,
            so be it.

If you fling me, as a skipping stone,
   hopping across the waters of time,
      I am given a brief leap and elation of flight
         often followed by a plunge to the depths.

The pebble accepts whichever fate...
   from lying unnoticed to a flight of ecstasy.
      It is better to be thankful for each moment of time,
         hopeful for the contact of attachments
            that might form, yet
               realizing the separateness
                  from an ultimate identity.

The struggle for significance
   is a personal quest,
      and while one often seeks the joy
         of a beholder's eye,
            neither moments nor centuries
               can determine the measure
                  of one's true worth and
                     essential value.

Death Wish

Knowing is a moment of enlightenment
        captured from the shadow of the night.

Gentleness is the steady rudder
        that guides through calm and storm.

Kindness is the state of giving
        to others without needing for oneself.

Needing is a characteristic of being human
        and not fully evolved.

Loving is joining another in an honest
        and shared embrace of life.

Living is having the knowledge to seek the way,
        the *kindness* to give it away,
        the *courage* to be gentle,
        the *humanness* to accept frailties,
        and *the openness* to love unconditionally.

Death cannot end the spirit that has formed
and extended beyond the body.

    Thank you for being a *very special Dad!*

                In memory of Dale C. Newton
                August 11, 1989

Life and Death

Yesterday, the messenger of death visited my house.
 Not the ominous angel of doom,
 But a memory of those I cherished before and after their exit,
 yet never was quite able to say the goodbye of appreciation
 and care that represented their life shared with me and others.

 Death can seem a cruel and heartless song that is
 difficult to sing with a harmony of life held dear,
 and the dissonance of not knowing how to let go...
 or to participate in the pain of their last days
 both physical and emotional.

 So, yesterday I felt tears of recognition
 much beyond the time that they were meant to have been.
 Emotions can be of both loss and love!
 This moment of knowing included a cancer
 eating away at my soul-felt inner hole of relationship
 still alive but with signs of a dying embers.

 My awareness wants to reach out and grasp the
 hand of the other to avoid the quicksand of slow death.
 At the same time, I feel her regret that she desires,
 even need to escape, as if my being is a wound
 and not a salve for embrace of a life shared.

 She indicates that I cannot understand what it
 is like from her inner self and personal wounds.
 Indeed, I feel caught in uncertainty of reaching out or
 letting go when my very presence seems
 to create as much affliction as assurance.

Part 4: FAMILY CONTRIBUTIONS

The following poems came from members of my family including three poems written by sons. Of special note are the two love sonnets written by my grandfather, Rev. Fredrick Graham Wright. I knew my grandfather when I was a child as we lived nearby in Irwin, Pennsylvania and he was the minister of our church. From that perspective, while kind and responsive, he was honored and respected as a learned minister. So, it was very humanizing to find these poems written when he was a college student. I was named after this grandfather and remember listening to Pirate baseball games in his study with the roll-top desk.

The Catcher

The catcher straddled the white rubber plate
with his greatest strength and stability.
His knees were bent like brass door hinges,
to make a brick wall
out of his five-foot, four-inch stature.

He was dressed head to toe in determination
and a gray baseball uniform.
A thick coat of Kansas soil outlined his purple numbers
and dug deep into the threads of his pants.
A quarter inch of molded plastic were his legs only defense
against a fury of flashing metal.

Two brown eyes were all that could be seen
within the shadows of his catcher's mask.
As the crowd cheered at a fast pace,
you could tell the catcher's mind was set
on only one thing in the world.

The way his pupils widened
showed that time had slowed down for him.
All his body movements were focused on one object;
a white sphere hurling through the air.

His eyes only wandered a fraction of a second
to see a runner thundering in his direction.
Beads of sweat fell like raindrops
from underneath his mask.

You could smell the anxiousness mixed in
with the salty aroma of sunflower seeds.
The ball skipped across the earth
and disappeared into an uproar of dust.

A pause blew across the diamond.
Then, like a victory flag from the trenches of a battlefield,
a rawhide glove arose from the dust
exposing a glimpse of chalky white leather with red stitching.

Mark Newton, August 22, 1998 (age 14)

44

LOYALTY

Should you be loyal to them
and forget the incident,
or quietly drift
away from them?

Some people say you can't
change people, and
that they have tried
many a time before.

But could you sleep
at night knowing
that your friends
you did ignore.

Why must they do
these things? Don't they
know I am confused as these
thoughts run through your head.

But your friends you
are afraid to lose;
one incident should change friendship,
that's the message I have to say.

Everyone makes mistakes
each and every day.
Forgiveness is the greatest tool,
use it to keep as many friends as you can.

Life is like a roller coaster
it has its up and downs.
Your life can change in an instant
for better or worse.

You cheat yourself by
following the group.
Liking things that are
not natural to you.

You follow that group
with loyalty.
You would die for them,
fight for them.

You strive to stay
a part of the group,
sometimes feeling like
a tag along.

But friends are the
most important thing
to you on the planet.
Without them you are alone.

When an incident happens
that makes you question your
loyalty toward your friends.
You are confused and worried.

Cherish your friends.
because a world
without friends it
is a cold and lonely world.

Daniel Newton, 1997

45

HOW DO I LOVE YOU?

Do I love you? Yes, I do.
For I love that you are tried and true,
To your home, to friends, the truest blue.
What more could I ask of one like you,
But that you love me too.

Love you? Must I tell you why.
'Tis because there's a sparkle in your eye,
Glowing fire of a soul that never will die.
Would that it might shine for me in reply
To the cry of my soul's sigh.

Love you? What does my heart reveal?
Your picture there so near I feel,
Conscious thoughts, that o'er me steal
Of you, at whose feet I suppliant kneel
For the gift of your love's seal.

Love you? Could help it if I would,
So kind and gentle, gracious and good,
So lovely and winsome in hat or hood,
If they face, form and virtues vanish should
My heart would faint for food.

Love you? How much? It's hard to say.
The world in the balance would not be pay.
Will you exchange, (happy then this day)
Your love for mine? O say me not nay
My heart yearns for aye and aye.

Written by Rev. F.G. Wright as a student of
English literature, Westminster College, 1898

VENUS

I.

O Venus morning star of love,
Thy brightness held full sway
When I awoke from dreams so sweet.
I scarcely her name repeat,
Lest they should fly away.

II.

So softly stole thy beams within
The chambers of my heart,
Love's day had dawned with rosy light
Ere I was conscious of my plight,
Or felt sly Cupid's dart.

III.

You knew I was a bachelor
Without a thought of love,
Content to live in fullest joy
The blissful life without alloy,
As angels do above.

IV.

And now you have disturbed my peace
Quietness of mind
Ere I do, wherever I be,
Her face, her eyes, her smile I see,
No happiness I find.

BACHELOR

V.

Now Venus, Goddess, star of love,
Come pay the debt you owe.
For ne'er before need I beware
of laughing eyes or curling hair,
or need to play the beau.

VI.

Come, tell me how I must begin
Her love and hand to gain.
For thou hast planted in my breast
A longing that can find no rest,
If longing it remain.

VII.

If that longed for day should come
Of happiness supreme:
Then unto thee my voice I'll raise
In anthem full of joyous praise,
And love shall be its theme.

VIII.

But if thy power cannot avail,
Nor help to me extend,
Bereft of peace, without a mate,
Then left to bare such cruel fate
I'll curses on the send.

This is a poem written in 1898 by the Reverent F. G. Wright,
my grandfather and father of Lois Wright Newton while he
was a student in college.

SOUL-CRAFT JOURNEYER'S PRAYER

The earth and the nature that lies therein is my shepherd,
It is the grounding of my soul into the truth that resides with all.

I enter by going into the green meadows carved between
the solid mountains of belief.

The waters of quiet springs and bubbling brooks nourish me,
there my soul is restored and brought back to the center.

I am guided by nature signals communicating
that I must use the sensors of my being.

Even though I walk through the valley of the shadow of death, I fear not
because there is great comfort in a world of harmony.

And, in the presence of fellow soul-craft journeyers I experience
a table of communion, as one, that supports the greater being.

Goodness and mercy anoint me as regrets and anxieties are left behind.
The loyal soldier departs from a protection that restricts the once uncertain child.

And now, I may walk forward into everyday life with the knowledge that
girds me from a detachment from my soul and true spirit of the natural world.

I must remember to wake quietly, live simply, and follow truth
and I shall live in the house of nature forever and ever.

Written 2003 at Completion of Vision Quest Journey
White Mountains, California
Fred B Newton

Unearthing My Place

By Douglas Newton

A beautiful question is this:

> *Where is my place that I am wont*
> *to give my whole heart and receive as much again?*

Grounding makes us aware of where we are.
Even this small yellowed leaf
resolute in its quivering descent
meets the earth with unmistakable heaviness,
a suddenness of place,
a hard stillness,
a communion with doubt.
The light but certain fall broken:
I am here now.

To the vulture above I say,
"I am alive, my heart bears longing.
The secret to death is living."

Beloved, come with me,
Move with me
on the land.
Feel its firmness,
smell its deliciousness.
Let me show you this wondrous place
we'll both enjoy.
It's a creek hidden
within the forest!

She said, "There is no crucifixion
without resurrection."
This said so certainly
like this dying leaf
hitting the ground
in front of me
shaking my bones,
announcing my life,
unearthing my place.

THIS DAY*

So here we meet in autumn
spring and summer both have passed.
To come is somber winter
when the days are overcast.

But now we lift our flagons
celebrate this life we live.
Let heavens hear our laughter
and the gods our sins forgive.

Tomorrow is uncertain,
yesterday of little need.
Today is all that matters
let the joyful times proceed.

And when my days have ended
put the ashes in an urn.
Pour a whiskey down the neck,
give the cap one final turn

Oh, do not mourn my passing
for you will travel there one day.
Just dance and sing and savor
every moment on the way.

*This poem was originally published in <u>Morning Daze</u> written
by my friend David Ullman. It seems an appropriate final work
to capture an appropriate end for any writing and a good life!